LEVEL 2

Harriet Tubman

Barbara Kramer

NATIONAL GEOGRAPHIC

Washington, D.C.

For my writers' group: Linda, Charlotte, and Katie. You keep me going! —B. K.

Copyright © 2020 National Geographic Partners, LLC

Published by National Geographic Partners, LLC, Washington, D.C. 20036. All rights reserved. Reproduction in whole or in part without written permission of the publisher is prohibited.

NATIONAL GEOGRAPHIC and Yellow Border Design are trademarks of the National Geographic Society, used under license.

Designed by YAY! Design

The author and publisher gratefully acknowledge the expert content review of this book by Kate Clifford Larson, historian and Harriet Tubman scholar, and author of *Bound for the Promised Land: Harriet Tubman, Portrait of an American Hero*; the literacy review of this book by Mariam Jean Dreher, professor of reading education, University of Maryland, College Park; and the sensitivity review of this book by Michele Mitchell, associate professor of history, New York University.

Publisher's Note
In recent years, the terminology related to slavery in America has been changing to better reflect the status of people held in bondage. Most academics now use the term "enslaved people" to communicate the lack of choice in their condition. In the context of an easy reader text, where the discussion is limited by vocabulary level and word count, we have chosen to use the historical term "slave" for the sake of clarity and readability for emerging readers.

The condition of enslaved peoples is a difficult subject to communicate in a book designed for early readers. Here, we mention that enslaved people were usually mistreated. You may wish to discuss the topic further with your young readers to help them better understand the concept of slavery.

Photo Credits
AS: Adobe Stock; ASP: Alamy Stock Photo; GI: Getty Images; GG: Granger/Granger.com; HAGI: Hulton Archive/Getty Images; NG: National Geographic Image Collection; SIG: Sarin Images/Granger.com; SS: Shutterstock
Cover: IanDagnall Computing/ASP; (BACKGROUND), David Coleman/ASP; 1, Alpha Historica/ASP; 3, Randy Duchaine/ASP; 4, Collection of the Library of Congress and the National Museum of African American History & Culture; 6, Mark Summerfield/ASP; 7, New York Historical Society/NG; 9, Herb Quick/ASP;

10 (UP), GG—All rights reserved; 10 (LO), HAGI;11 (UP), SIG—All rights reserved; 11 (CTR), HAGI; 12, spiritofamerica/AS; 14, Focus Features/Entertainment Pictures/ASP; 15, Everett Historical/SS; 16, Daniel Borzynski/ASP; 17, Schomburg Center for Research in Black Culture, Manuscripts, Archives and Rare Books Division, The New York Public Library; 18, GG—All rights reserved; 19 (UP), Jim Gensheimer/NG; 19 (LO), Harriet Tubman, 2005 (digital), Frey, Matthew (b.1974)/Private Collection/Wood Ronsaville Harlin, Inc. USA/Bridgeman Images; 20, GG—All rights reserved; 21 (UP), Courtesy of the Delaware Historical Society; 21 (LO), Photos.com/GI; 22 (UP), Jerry Pinkney/NG; 22 (CTR), Gerald Martineau/The Washington Post/GI; 22 (LO LE), spatuletail/SS; 22 (LO RT), Time Life Pictures/US Postal Service/The LIFE Picture Collection/GI; 23 (UP), Collection of the Smithsonian National Museum of African American History and Culture, Gift of Charles L. Blockson; 23 (CTR), stockelements/SS; 23 (LO), Zack Frank/AS; 25, Harriet Tubman. Portrait. African-American abolitionist and Union spy during the American Civil War/British Library, London, UK/© British Library Board. All Rights Reserved/Bridgeman Images; 26, Debra Millet/SS; 26-27 (LO), sharpner/SS; 27, GG—All rights reserved; 28, Ira Block/NG; 28-29 (LO), sharpner/SS; 29, GHI/Universal History Archive via GI; 30 (UP), Edwin Remsburg/VW Pics via GI; 30 (CTR), The Print Collector/GI; 30 (LO), Everett Historical/SS; 31 (UP LE), guteksk7/SS; 31 (UP RT), SIG—All rights reserved; 31 (LO LE), Exodus I: Black Moses (Harriet Tubman), 1951 (linocut), White, Charles Wilbert (1918-79)/Philadelphia Museum of Art, Pennsylvania, PA, USA/Bequest of Mrs. Rose Weiss, 2009/Bridgeman Images; 31 (LO RT), SIG—All rights reserved; 32 (UP RT), HAGI; 32 (CTR LE), Bettmann/GI; 32 (CTR RT), Winfield Parks/NG; 32 (LO LE), Schomburg Center for Research in Black Culture, Manuscripts, Archives and Rare Books Division, The New York Public Library; 32 (LO RT), SIG—All rights reserved; header (THROUGHOUT), Beautiful landscape/SS; "Word to Know" (THROUGHOUT), Randy Duchaine/ASP

Library of Congress Cataloging-in-Publication Data
Names: Kramer, Barbara, author.
Title: Harriet Tubman / by Barbara Kramer.
Description: Washington, DC : National Geographic Kids, 2020. | Series: National Geographic Readers
Identifiers: LCCN 2019008867 (print) | LCCN 2019010703 (ebook) | ISBN 9781426337239 (e-book) | ISBN 9781426337246 (e-book) | ISBN 9781426337215 (pbk.) | ISBN 9781426337222 (hardcover)
Subjects: LCSH: Tubman, Harriet, 1822-1913--Juvenile literature. | Slaves--United States--Biography--Juvenile literature. | African American women--Biography--Juvenile literature. | African Americans--Biography--Juvenile literature. | Underground Railroad--Juvenile literature.
Classification: LCC E444.T82 (ebook) | LCC E444.T82 K725 2020 (print) | DDC 326/.8092 [B] --dc23
LC record available at https://lccn.loc.gov/2019008867

National Geographic supports K–12 educators with ELA Common Core Resources. Visit natgeoed.org/commoncore for more information.

Printed in the United States of America
19/WOR/1

Table of Contents

Who Was Harriet Tubman?	4
A Girl Called Minty	6
In Her Time	10
Escape!	12
Helping Others	18
6 Cool Facts About Harriet Tubman	22
A Secret Spy	24
More Work to Do	26
Quiz Whiz	30
Glossary	32

Who Was Harriet Tubman?

Harriet Tubman when she was about 46 years old

Harriet Tubman was born a slave. This meant she was not free. Even as a child, she had to work hard for her owner, or master. She had to do as she was told. She could not leave his farm.

As a young woman, Harriet made a daring escape to freedom. Then she put her own life in danger again to lead other slaves to freedom. She is a hero to many for being so brave.

Word to Know

SLAVE: A person who was considered to be property and was owned by another person. A slave had to work for no pay and was usually mistreated.

A Girl Called Minty

Harriet Tubman was born in Dorchester County, Maryland, U.S.A., around 1822. Her parents named her Araminta (air-a-MINT-a). They called her "Minty." Later, she changed her name to Harriet. Harriet was also her mother's name.

Harriet and her eight brothers and sisters spent their early years in a cabin much like this one.

That's a FACT! No one knows Harriet's exact birth date. Her parents could not record it because they could not read or write.

Slaves worked long hours on the farm.

When Harriet was about six years old, her master sent her away to work on other farms. She cleaned houses and later worked in the fields. At night, she cried because she missed her family.

In Her Own Words

"I used to sleep on the floor ... and there I'd lie and cry and cry."

One day when Harriet was a teenager, she went to the store for supplies. There was another slave at the store. He ran from an overseer (OH-vur-see-ur). The overseer grabbed a two-pound weight from the counter and threw it at the fleeing boy. It missed him and hit Harriet in the head instead.

For the rest of her life, Harriet had terrible headaches. She also fell asleep suddenly, even when she was talking or working.

Word to Know

OVERSEER: A person who was in charge of a master's slaves

Harriet was badly hurt at this village store in Bucktown, Maryland. It is now a museum.

In Her Time

In the 1820s, growing up as a slave was very different from growing up as a child who was free.

SCHOOL: Slaves could not attend school. Teaching them to read or write was against the law in some states. An education would give them power.

HOME: Slaves lived in small cabins with dirt floors. Whole families were crowded into one room. They often had no beds, so they slept on straw on the floor.

UNDERGROUND RAILROAD: Some slaves escaped from their masters through the Underground Railroad. The people who led them to safety were called conductors.

RIGHTS: Slaves had no rights and were usually mistreated. They were listed as property along with their owner's animals. They could be sold to other masters to work without pay at any time. Children were often taken from their parents to be sold.

Words to Know

UNDERGROUND RAILROAD: Not a real railroad, but a secret network of people who helped slaves escape to freedom

RIGHTS: Basic freedoms protected by law, such as the right to live, learn, and work as one chooses

Escape!

In 1844, Harriet married John Tubman, a free black man. She dreamed of being free, too.

The Mason-Dixon Line marked the border between the slave state of Maryland and the free state of Pennsylvania. But in time, that name came to stand for the dividing line between all slave and free states.

At that time, the United States was divided. There were free states in the North and slave states in the South. Harriet wanted to escape to a free state, but John would not go with her. It was against the law to help a slave escape.

Word to Know

FREE STATE: A U.S. state that did not allow people to own slaves

An actress playing Harriet Tubman in a movie about her life

In 1849, Tubman learned that she was going to be sold by her master. So she made a plan to escape.

One night when everyone was sleeping, Tubman crept out of her cabin. She went to the home of a white woman, who hid her. The woman also gave Tubman the names of others who would help. Tubman was now on her way north using the Underground Railroad.

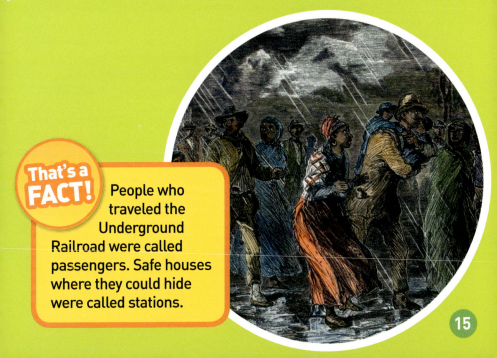

That's a FACT! People who traveled the Underground Railroad were called passengers. Safe houses where they could hide were called stations.

Tubman traveled at night. It was easier to hide

Word to Know

SLAVE CATCHERS: Men who were paid rewards to find escaped slaves and return them to their masters

from slave catchers in the dark. One night, a man let her ride in the back of his wagon. Most of the time, Tubman walked. She traveled 90 miles north to Pennsylvania, U.S.A.

While making their way to freedom, people sometimes hid in the back of a wagon. They were covered with straw or grain bags so no one would see them.

In 1849, there was a law that said owners could take back their slaves, even from free states.

Tubman could live and work as a free person in that state. But there was still danger. Slave catchers could find her and take her back to her master.

In Her Own Words

"I looked at my hands to see if I was the same person now that I was free."

Helping Others

Philadelphia, Pennsylvania, in 1850

Tubman went to Philadelphia. She cleaned homes and worked as a cook at a hotel. But she could not stop thinking about her family. She wanted them to be free, too. So she became a conductor on the Underground Railroad.

In Her Own Words

"My home, after all, was ... with the old folks, and my brothers and sisters ... I was free, and they should be free also."

Her first rescue was in December 1850. Tubman's niece and her niece's two children were about to be sold. Tubman helped them escape.

This drawing shows Tubman leading others to freedom.

In the spring of 1851, Tubman led one of her brothers and two other people to safety. Later, she helped her parents and other family members escape. Each trip meant danger for Tubman. Slave catchers were looking for her. But fear did not stop her.

This church in Pennsylvania served as a station on the Underground Railroad.

That's a FACT! Tubman fooled some slave catchers by holding up a newspaper like she was reading it. They knew she couldn't read, so they walked right past her.

Tubman's master posted a notice in the newspaper offering $100 for her return. Today, that would be like offering more than $3,000.

From 1850 to 1860, Tubman made a total of 13 trips back to Maryland. She bravely led about 70 people to freedom.

In Her Own Words

"I can say what most conductors can't say—I never ran my train off the track and I never lost a passenger."

6 COOL FACTS About Harriet Tubman

1. Tubman earned the nickname Moses for her work as a conductor on the Underground Railroad. Moses was a man who led his people to freedom from slavery in ancient Egypt.

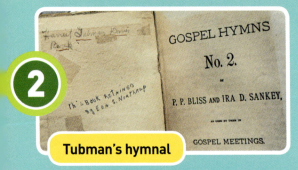

Tubman's hymnal

2. Tubman used music to send secret signals to the people she led to freedom. When she sang a song such as "Bound for the Promised Land," they knew it was time to leave.

3. Tubman was honored with two U.S. postage stamps, in 1978 and 1995. And in 2016, when leaders wanted to change the face on the $20 bill, Tubman was the favorite choice.

4 People around the world admired Tubman. In 1897, Queen Victoria of England gave Tubman a silver medal and a silk lace shawl.

5 Later in her life, Tubman worked for equal rights for women. She gave speeches about her life and about fair treatment of all people.

This statue of Tubman stands in the Harlem area of New York City.

Two national parks honor Tubman and her work: the Harriet Tubman Underground Railroad National Historical Park in Maryland and the Harriet Tubman National Historical Park in New York, U.S.A.

6 In 1859, Tubman moved from Pennsylvania to this home in Auburn, New York. It's now part of the Harriet Tubman National Historical Park.

A Secret Spy

In 1861, the Civil War began between free states in the North and slave states in the South. Tubman believed the war would lead to freedom for slaves. She wanted to help.

She worked as a nurse to Northern soldiers. She was also a spy. She would sneak behind enemy lines to gather information for the North. No one took notice of a woman who seemed to be just another slave.

Tubman helped soldiers from the North during the Civil War.

That's a FACT!

In June 1863, Tubman led a surprise military attack in South Carolina, freeing more than 750 slaves. She was the first woman to lead a Civil War raid.

HARRIET TUBMAN.

More Work to Do

This is the city of Auburn, New York, as it appears today.

After the war, Tubman went home to Auburn, New York. She had lived there since 1859. Her parents lived with her. Her home was also a place where newly free people could go.

1822
Born around this time in Dorchester County, Maryland

1835
Suffers a serious head injury

1844
Marries John Tubman

Tubman's husband, John, never did join her in the North. He died in 1867. Two years later, she married Nelson Davis. They adopted a daughter, Gertie.

Tubman (left) with Nelson and their daughter, Gertie

1849
Escapes to freedom

1850
Becomes a conductor on the Underground Railroad

1859
Buys her own home in Auburn, New York

Today, the Harriet Tubman Home for the Aged is a National Historic Landmark that people can visit.

In 1908, Tubman opened a home in Auburn for elderly African Americans. She moved into the home herself when her health began to fail. Tubman died on March 10, 1913. She was about 91 years old.

1862–1864
Works as a nurse and spy for the North during the Civil War

1869
Marries Nelson Davis

1874
Adopts a daughter, Gertie

Tubman was brave and kind. Today, her story inspires many people to fight for equal rights and to always help others.

Tubman in 1911, when she was about 89 years old

1880s
Becomes active in the fight for equal rights for women, including the right to vote

1908
Opens the Harriet Tubman Home for the Aged

1913
Dies on March 10

QUIZ WHIZ

How much do you know about Harriet Tubman? After reading this book, probably a lot! Take this quiz and find out.

Answers are at the bottom of page 31.

In what state was Tubman born?

A. Pennsylvania
B. New York
C. Maryland
D. South Carolina

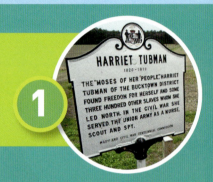

Which of these health problems were caused by Tubman's head injury?

A. She had trouble walking.
B. Her eyesight got worse.
C. She had trouble hearing.
D. She fell asleep suddenly.

A person who led slaves to freedom on the Underground Railroad was called _____.

A. a conductor
B. a passenger
C. a slave catcher
D. an overseer

4

Why did Tubman travel at night when she was escaping from slavery?

A. She had to work during the day.
B. It was easier to hide in the dark.
C. The sun was too hot during the day.
D. She could see better at night.

States that did not allow people to own slaves were called _____.

A. stations
B. slave states
C. safe states
D. free states

5

Tubman led about _____ people to freedom on the Underground Railroad.

A. 40
B. 70
C. 150
D. 750

6

How did Tubman help the North during the Civil War?

A. She was a nurse to the soldiers.
B. She worked as a spy.
C. She led a surprise attack in South Carolina.
D. All of the above.

7

Answers: 1. C, 2. D, 3. A, 4. B, 5. D, 6. B, 7. D

FREE STATE: A U.S. state that did not allow people to own slaves

OVERSEER: A person who was in charge of a master's slaves

RIGHTS: Basic freedoms protected by law, such as the right to live, learn, and work as one chooses

SLAVE: A person who was considered to be property and was owned by another person

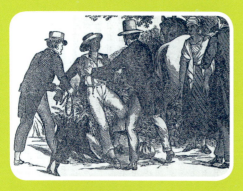

SLAVE CATCHERS: Men who were paid rewards to find escaped slaves and return them to their masters

UNDERGROUND RAILROAD: Not a real railroad, but a secret network of people who helped slaves escape to freedom